7/6 NET

# SO EASY TO LOVE

To those who are trying to pray but who find it more difficult than they have been led to suppose, to those who want to know something of well-tried ways of praying, and to those who want to learn how to overcome distractions in prayer, this small book will be most welcome.

Brother Roger describes here a way of prayer which he has found helpful and which may be of use in helping others to come nearer to God. It is based on Madame Guyon's famous *Moyen Court*, and the author has expressed in a modern idiom what she might have written had she lived today, while trying to avoid the mistakes she made.

Here are some of the chapter headings:

Prayer is for Everyone

When Nothing Seems to Happen

Thinking About Jesus

What About a Hair Shirt?

Active Peace

We Have to Listen If We Want to Pray

What God Sees in Us

The Bad Patch

Trouble

The Lively Sacrifice

What Happens

How Dull Are the Services at Your Church?

*Titles in this format:*

*Anon.—The Book of the Poor in Spirit
Anon.—They Speak By Silences
Bowden—The Dazzling Darkness
*Camus—The Spirit of St. François de Sales
*De Sales—Introduction to the Devout Life
*De Sales—Spiritual Maxims (ed. Kelley)
Fisher—Anthology of Prayers
*Guardini { The Rosary of Our Lady
           The Living God (in one volume)
*Guardini—Before Mass
Hancock—Red Letter Days
Julian of Norwich—A Shewing of God's Love (ed. Reynolds)
McSorley—Think and Pray
Newman—Meditations and Devotions
Roger, C.R.—So Easy to Love
*Schryvers—The Gift of Oneself
Underhill { The School of Charity
           The Mystery of Sacrifice (in one volume)
Underhill { The Fruits of the Spirit
           Light of Christ
           Abba (in one volume)
*Winzen—Symbols of Christ

\* not for sale in U.S.A. and Canada

# SO EASY TO LOVE

BROTHER ROGER, C.R.

LONGMANS, GREEN AND CO
LONDON · NEW YORK · TORONTO

LONGMANS, GREEN AND CO LTD
6 & 7 CLIFFORD STREET LONDON W I
THIBAULT HOUSE THIBAULT SQUARE CAPE TOWN
605–611 LONSDALE STREET MELBOURNE C I

LONGMANS, GREEN AND CO INC
55 FIFTH AVENUE NEW YORK 3

LONGMANS, GREEN AND CO
20 CRANFIELD ROAD TORONTO 16

ORIENT LONGMANS PRIVATE LTD
CALCUTTA BOMBAY MADRAS
DELHI HYDERABAD DACCA

© 

*Brother Roger Castle*, 1957

*First Published* 1957

PRINTED IN GREAT BRITAIN BY BLACKIE & SON, LTD., AT
THE VILLAFIELD PRESS, BISHOPBRIGGS, GLASGOW

# PREFACE

After reading Count Michael de la Bedoyère's *The Archbishop and the Lady*, which is an account of the controversy between Fénélon and Bossuet over the teaching of Madame Guyon, who was condemned as a Quietist, I came to the conclusion that I had been praying like Madame Guyon all my Christian life. So I went to the sources, and read Madame Guyon's autobiography, her *Moyen Court* and her *Les Torrens Spirituels*.

It is easy to see why she was condemned. She did not express herself very well. But her life must have been the fruit of her prayer, and that strikes one as having been pretty exemplary.

This little book of mine owes practically everything to the *Moyen Court*, but is also an attempt to express in a modern idiom what I think she meant, judging from her life.

I expect the rest of the book is full of 'borrowings'. If it is they are things I have made so much my own that I do not now know where I 'borrowed' them from. But I am very grateful to the people who 'lent' them to me.

# CONTENTS

# Contents

# INTRODUCTION

Prayer is not the easy way of getting what you want; but it is the only way of becoming what God wants you to be: he wants you to be perfect, like him.

Jesus did say, 'Ye shall seek after me and ye shall not find me' (John 7 : 34), but he who cannot contradict himself also said, 'Seek and ye shall find' (Matthew 7 : 7). If you try to find God, so as to discover what he wants you to be like, and are not prepared to give up all your sins—even your favourite ones—you will never find him. You are not going about it the right way; so he added, 'Ye shall die in your sins' (John 8 : 21). But if you look for God in your heart, and, so as to be able to recognize him, you do give up all your sins, you cannot help but find him.

The way of prayer looks so formidable, and the spirit of prayer so difficult to come by, that most people are put off, and make not the slightest effort to do anything about it.

Anything worth doing has its difficulties, and they are overcome or not according to whether we hope or despair.

If we realize how good God is to us, and how much he longs to be with us, we should not allow imaginary difficulties, or any difficulties for that matter, to put us off. 'He who did not shield his own Son, but gave him up for us all—can we not trust such a God to give us, with him, everything else we need?' (Romans 8 : 32 : J. B. Phillips.) We are courageous and persevering in the things of this world, but we give up when it comes to the 'one thing needful' (Luke 10 : 42).

If you think that God is difficult to find—all right; but just try, and experience may convince you that the reality is something far beyond anything you have ever known.

Prayer is children going to the Father, who loves to see them come to him full of trust; and is grieved when they cannot trust, or do not know how to show their love. It is just simply doing what Our Lord did. If you are prepared to try to give up your sins, then this is the easy way to the love of God.

Jesus loves simplicity and innocence, and delights to 'dwell with the children of men'

(Proverbs 8 : 31); with those men who are ready to become as little children. He will lead them to look for him within themselves, where he is just as certainly as he once was in the manger, waiting for them to show him their love, so that he may show them his. He knows how to rouse and attract and convert. He knows how to make himself heard, experienced and beloved. Let him try on you.

# I

## PRAYER IS FOR EVERYONE

# PRAYER IS FOR EVERYONE

MOST people think that prayer is not for them. As a matter of fact, everyone can pray; and all are called to pray, as everyone can find salvation, and all are called to be saved.

Prayer is the offering of the heart to God, and an effort to love (1 Thes. 5 : 17). S. Paul tells us to pray without ceasing, and Our Lord said, "I say unto you all, watch and pray" (Mark 13 : 33 : 37).

The sort of prayer which is really preaching oneself a sermon may not suit everyone. But we all know we ought to live by love, and we cannot do that unless we try to focus our attention on the Object of love.

This is the prayer for everyone, however wretched, however far off, however dull or ignorant or stupid. The Father longs to hold you in his arms, and the Son called especially the unlikely ones to come to him.

The only ones who are not invited are the heartless. There must be a heart if there is to be love. We all have hearts. The trouble is we do not know how to give them.

All who want to pray, can pray.

Prayer can make us perfect, for the way to perfection is to walk in the presence of God, for he himself said, "walk before me, and be thou perfect" (Gen. 17 : 1). Prayer brings us into his presence and keeps us there.

Your way of getting to God must be your own way, not someone else's. It must fit in with your environment. It must be truly yours, like a suit made to measure.

Prayer cannot come only from the brain, and it must come from the heart. We can only think of one thing at a time, but we can love all the time, whatever we are doing.

Nothing can disturb prayer that comes from the heart, except the wrong sort of love; and when once you have experienced God and the reality of his love, no other loves seem worth bothering about, and all other loves are included in it.

God is so easily possessed and enjoyed, because "in him we live, and move, and have our being" (Acts 17 : 28). He wants to give himself to us more than we can possibly want to receive him. It all depends on how you go about it. The right way is easier than breathing. However incapable you think you are of reaching the heights of prayer, you can, if you try, live with God with as little effort and interruption as you live in the world.

# II

# THE METHOD

# THE METHOD

THE best way to begin to pray is by meditative reading, and by thinking about God.

If you try meditative reading, the thing to do is to take one of the gospels, and read just a little of it. Read until you find something that applies to you and to your special relationship with God. Read only a very little, and read that little over and over again, until there is nothing more left for you at the moment.

If you have time, read another little bit, and do just as you did before.

Some people find the Authorized Version difficult to get on with. If you do, try reading the Penguin edition of The Four Gospels. Some people find J. B. Phillips's *Letters to Young Churches* a useful book to read meditatively. It is a fluent and modern translation of all the

Epistles in the New Testament. Any book at all about God will do.

It is not good to read fast; nor is it good to read much. You are not studying; you are trying to get into the mood to approach God.

If you try just thinking about God, you are meditating. We do not find it difficult to meditate on someone we are attracted by, or on some matter that interests us deeply. They occupy our minds most of the day. We meditate on them most of the day.

To meditate on God, you should make a great effort to believe that he is with you. He has always been with you, from the time you were born. He came to you in a special way when you were christened. He will be with you till you die. He will never leave you, whatever you do, however much you sin. He may not be able to live his life in you as he longs to, but he will be there waiting, as it were. He does not come into your soul; he is already there. This is grace, the free Gift, the Holy Thing given to us at our baptism. It is nothing we have ever deserved. It is grace—gratis—free.

2

Then, since he is with you, think of something you know about him, or of something he did during the time he lived on earth as Man. Do not reason about him, just let your mind rest on him. Fix your attention on him. What you are trying to do is to be always in his presence. The matter you have chosen as the subject of your meditation should have more or less the same use as a photograph of your beloved. It is something for you to focus your love upon.

If you do this, you will find that the certainty of God present within you will produce a turning inwards of your whole self, which will keep your thoughts from wandering. The more real the presence of God in your soul becomes to you, the less chance will there be of distractions.

He did promise that he would come and make his abode with the man that loved him (John 14 : 23).

When you do for a moment find that you are really turned in towards God in your soul, and are filled with the certainty of his presence within you, when your senses are all at rest, and when you find you have come to the fringe of yourself and are in the real and silent centre, with the mind filled with whatever it is you have chosen for your subject, do not reason, just try to love, and do not try to force the moment to stay; if you do, you will only drive it away. Try to enjoy it to the full—this little experience of Reality, and try to take it along with you when you have to go on living in the world. Your soul after such an exercise should be still and at rest, full of respect, trust and love. You ought to be wonderful to meet.

This little way is a vital necessity, and will make your soul grow very quickly.

When you meditate, you are trying, in the first place, to look at God, but you will also have to keep an eye on your senses. They distract one so; and if you tussle with them, they only get worse. I believe the only satisfactory way to drive them off, is to keep on turning inwards to the real presence of God within your soul.

This turning away from your distractions, and in towards the Real Presence, may take up the whole of your time of meditation. There are times when it certainly will; and the times may be very long.

Do not wander from subject to subject. Choose one subject for your meditation and stick to it. When there is nothing left for you to meditate on, your meditation is finished, and you will have to spend the rest of your time trying to love, and turning in towards the God within you.

The soul spends so much of its time away from home, that it does find it difficult and trying to be in, even to be with its God; but as it gets accustomed to staying in, little by little it will begin to enjoy it. There is nothing so absorbing as the experience of the presence of God communicating himself to his creature.

# III

## A STEP ALONG THE WAY

# A STEP ALONG THE WAY

JESUS CHRIST said, "Without me you can do nothing" (John 15 : 5). He did not say without his teaching, nor without reading the Bible, nor without keeping the Ten Commandments, nor without being 'sober and respectable'; though all these things are very necessary. But he did say, "Without me—me myself, you can do nothing."

So the first step must be to learn the fundamental truth that "the kingdom of God is within you" (Luke 17 : 21).

You must begin by worshipping and adoring God, with the eyes of your head closed, but the eyes of your soul open. Then tell him how certainly you believe that he is present within you, and with all the determination you are capable of, stay in the Presence; which means keeping that eye on your wandering senses.

Suppose you were not in a situation where you were able to take up a book and read, you might easily use the Lord's Prayer as a focusing point for your meditation: dwelling on the idea of *Our Father*, asking him for what you need, loving the very sound of the name, staying with him in respectful silence, waiting to know what he wants you to do.

Or take your knocks and wretchednesses to him, show him the dirt that he can so easily wash off; tell him how ashamed of yourself you are; tell him how much you love him all the same, and stay quiet to see what plan he has for your improvement.

Or go to the King of Glory and admit his claim to rule over you. Tell him how much you love and honour him, and wait in silent attention for his orders.

Then, if you can, rest there in silence, until you feel you need more material for loving; then go on to the next part: *Thy will be done on earth as it is in heaven*. Surrender yourself into his hands. Tell him, and mean it, that you are content to do and be what he wants. Tell him you are offering yourself because you love, and tell him that all you want in return is love.

Anything we imagine about the Presence of God must be wrong. There is hardly anything we say about him that is absolutely true. Words work very uncertainly when they have to do with God. But we can picture Jesus to ourselves. We can have ideas about the events of his life on earth. Find these, if you will, in the silent centre.

When we have been allowed an experience of the Presence, there is another step to take; not necessarily a second step, one following on the first, but another. It may have been your first. It is not a step up, nor a better, stronger step. It is just another.

# IV

## ANOTHER STEP

## ANOTHER STEP

THIS step does not necessarily come after the one described in the last chapter, nor is it necessarily better or more advanced; it is just another step.

You personally may find it easy to get near to God, and to remember that you are always in his presence; and you may enjoy easy, pleasant prayers.

If you are like this, then, as soon as you have started your special prayer-time by knowing that you are in the presence of God, remain there knowing this for a while; remain there, in fact, until you feel you are slipping away from his presence. When you feel the smallest wandering of the attention, say some loving word: just tell God you love him, in any words that come into your mind; then, if you find yourself back in his presence, stay there.

Do not be disturbed at not being able to stay

with him as long as you would like to; just un-
hurriedly and gently get back where you would
be, by quiet, loving words.

Directly you know you are back with God,
stop all efforts to say things, unless you think
God wants you to.

It is a good plan never to end your special
time of prayer without a moment or two of
silence.

It is also very important to begin your special
time of prayer courageously: being quite ready
to take whatever God has prepared for you. It
may be he will have great sweetness and joy for
you; but it may equally well be that he has
prepared for you nothing but weariness and
distraction.

We only go to our prayer because we want to
love, not because we want comfort. Our love
must be pure—quite disinterested. We are there
in his presence waiting to do whatever he wants
us to do.

If you go in this frame of mind, you will never be disappointed nor surprised, only expectant.

# V

## WHEN NOTHING SEEMS TO HAPPEN

# WHEN NOTHING SEEMS TO HAPPEN

GOD is always with the soul that loves, but sometimes he may seem to leave us to ourselves. He never does, but he may sometimes allow us to think we are deserted by him. Perhaps he does this because we have been getting slack, perhaps because he wants us to look for him in faith and pure love.

We cannot guess what the rewards of our faith and love may be. Sometimes the so-called coincidences that turn out to be so useful, are his rewards.

He never allows us to give him anything without returning it a hundredfold. He promised it. (Mark 10 : 30.)

At the times when you think he has left you, do not worry and distress yourself and struggle to get him back. No exertion of yours will hurry what you think is his return. All you have to do is to resign yourself to his apparent absence, waiting patiently and lovingly, knowing that we deserve nothing of him, but longing for him, in silence and hope and deep respect.

In this way you will show him that you want nothing but what he wants. You only want him, not your own selfish desires, not the delights of your senses.

This way of behaving is the one that pleases best the heart of Jesus, and, if anything will, it is this that will bring the assurance of his presence back to you.

# VI

## SURRENDER

# SURRENDER

WHEN we have got as far as to be able to take the apparent absence of God as being something good in itself, we are getting to the time when we ought to be able to consider the possibility of giving ourselves entirely into God's hands.

The present moment shows us what God wants us to do now; and when we believe this, we shall know that everything that happens is from God, and that he uses people as his tools.

The things that happen to us do not really come from people; they come from God. Therefore they are good, whatever they may seem to be.

Knowing this, you give the whole of yourself to God. And whatever happens, do not take yourself back again. Having given yourself, you have no further rights over yourself.

When we can give ourselves to God, we are on the right way to perfection.

Surrender does not mean that we no longer use our reason or our common sense; but it does mean that we use them always with God. We, too, are his tools, just as certainly as are the people with whom we have to deal. Only perhaps some of them are his unwitting tools; we shall know what is happening to us, or at least we shall have the certain assurance that we are doing what God wants.

We shall not need to fuss and bother any more; we are at God's disposal, waiting to be used. "Take no thought for the morrow; for the morrow shall take thought for the things of itself" (Matthew 6 : 34), if you have first sought God and his righteousness.

Surrender of self applies as much to the daily affairs of life as it does to the affairs of the soul. They cannot be separated. We are all of a piece.

Every time you think of doing what you want

to do, think if God wants it too. He may; but again, he may not. In which case, you simply must not do it. If you are doubtful about it, still do not do it. Only do what you are certain he requires you to do now.

Do not bother about the past; it is past. And leave what is to come to God. The present moment is your concern. See that it is a part of the splendid orderliness of God.

The present moment is always an infallible indication of what God wants you to do now. It is possible he may only want you to be undecided.

Everything comes from our good Father, except our sins. They never do.

It is strange that we should have to plan how to surrender ourselves to God, when we know so well how to do it to a person. The surrender to the beloved person is the same surrender (only it works out so wonderfully different) as the one we make to God. If you want to learn how, let yourself go in love, and you will see the simplicity of it.

You do not do things you know your human beloved would not want you to do. You would not do anything that you would think he might possibly dislike. Treat the Divine Beloved in the same way.

If you are undemonstrative, do your best; love slowly, and wait patiently till Love makes himself beloved in his own way.

# VII

## SUFFERING

# SUFFERING

BE content with whatever God does with you. If you love him for himself alone, you will be just as pleased to find him on Calvary as on the Mountain of the Transfiguration.

Do not look for him on the one and hide from him on the other. Do not delight in caresses, and run away from crucifixion; nor when crucifixion does come, turn to someone for comfort.

There is no comfort anywhere else, but in the very thing God sends us. It is impossible to love God and not the way he uses us. God gives us whatever he thinks best, and what he gives us gives us God.

When you begin to dread what you see is coming to you, turn in towards God, and offer yourself in sacrifice. Then, because you take it willingly, and are ready for it, the burden will not be so heavy. This does not mean that it will not be heavy. It is no cross at all unless you feel it; but anticipation plays a big part in most of our sufferings. Remember that Jesus Christ was willing to suffer to the uttermost, if it was his Father's will. He feared what was coming to him, and loathed it, but he took it.

Sometimes you will fall under your cross. Jesus did three times. Sometimes you will bear it with strength and vigour. It should be all the same to you. It is how God wants you to bear it.

# VIII

## THINKING ABOUT JESUS

# THINKING ABOUT JESUS

IT may seem that this way of prayer does not take sufficiently into account the various events of Our Lord's life on earth; but anyone who is trying to abandon himself to God is following the way which is Jesus, listening to the truth which is Jesus, and living a life which is Jesus. (John 14 : 6.)

We must be soaked in the Gospel. You should have a copy of at least one of the gospels in your pocket or in your bag. You can read the Penguin Four Gospels anywhere, and no one will know what you are doing.

But to live through the various states of Jesus Christ is far better than only reading about them.

When we were baptised, we became a part of the Body of Christ, called to live our own little bit of the Incarnate Life of God perpetuated here on earth. That is the vocation of every member of the Church.

Our Lord still carries on his ministry, still heals, still lives through his Passion and Resurrection in and through his Church; and his Church is you and me.

The reason why the Church is not as effectual as it ought to be is because Christians do not live up to their vocation. The Church in the Acts of the Apostles seems very different from the Church as we know it now. To say that the Body of Christ is old and tired sounds like blasphemy. Perhaps a soul that is old and tired is a blasphemy: something, that is, that is profane and impious.

Sometimes God makes one of his lovers live through in a special way one of his own mysterious states. There are people whose lives have been real replicas of the Holy Childhood; some have lived through long Gethsemanes, some have known the Passion, others have lived Resurrection and Pentecostal lives—lives on fire with the Holy Spirit.

God will certainly ask us to live out some part of his life; it is our business to reach out to him for it, to dwell in him, and sink to nothingness before his terrifying love. We must take whatever he offers: darkness or light, usefulness or uselessness, strength or weakness, delight or disgust, temptations, distractions, pain, weariness, doubts; and they will all lead us to him.

It does not matter in the slightest if some parts of Our Lord's life seem to have very little meaning or attraction for us. Since we love God, we love all of him. If we are united to God, we are united to all of him. We shall understand it all in the end.

# IX

## GOODNESS

# GOODNESS

When you are united to God, you will see how easy it is to be good.

When we have God, we have everything; and the closer we get to God, astonishing as it may seem, the more like him we shall grow.

It is fairly easy to look good, and seem good, but it is only when we are close to God within us that we are good. That is real fundamental and lasting good.

You cannot help being good then. You certainly will not think you are. But God will make you good. He will be very jealous of you, and you will find that, sooner or later, nothing gives you any satisfaction but him and his will.

You will be one of those who are ready to take that terrifying blind jump into God's arms, which you believe and know are waiting to catch you and carry you to unknown but certain goodness by unknown, terrifying but sure ways. You know and believe, but still the jump is just as terrifying as if you did not know and believe.

If we all jumped, the world would be a very different place. It is only love that is needed. "Love, and then do what you please", as St. Augustine said. It is true, for when we love, we would do anything rather than offend our love; but it so depends upon whether our love is Love.

# X

## WHAT ABOUT HAIR SHIRTS?

# WHAT ABOUT HAIR SHIRTS?

Unless we are afraid of offending Love, we shall never get control over our senses and our passions.

You may think that the senses and passions control your soul, but it is the other way round.

The more we try by purely physical means to keep our senses under, the busier will our souls be, and the farther away from their still centres. They will be thinking of the senses, and a soul occupied with the senses stimulates them, and they in their turn stimulate the desires.

Try to keep at the still centre of your soul where God is. This is the best way to keep the desires in order. They will grow to be like God's —or perhaps it would be nearer the truth to say you will only desire what God wants you to desire.

God will provide you with all the discipline you need. If he thinks good, he will give you someone to direct you, who will see that you get what is good for you.

Everyone who tries to pray needs discipline; but looking for mortification is not a fruitful spiritual exercise.

If we are close to God, our senses will not run away with us. He will keep us close to him, and discipline everything in us that needs to be disciplined. That is the price of throwing oneself into the arms of God.

There are certain little mortifications, however, that do no harm to anyone—not even to the feeblest in health. Anyone, however delicate, can be careful of what he listens to and looks at.

God who is Beauty as well as Love, can fill the mind with beauty, if we will leave it to him. Strange to say, our taste may not improve, but we shall not want to hear or see what is fundamentally bad.

If we are close to God, we are as far as we can be from sin. If we stay there, we are converted —permanently turned towards God.

# XI

## CONVERSION

# CONVERSION

WHEN we are completely converted, we are completely turned towards God. Conversion does not only mean that now we like to go to church, when before we didn't.

To be saved we must give up sin, and find our true pleasure in goodness. But even this is not complete conversion. Turning to God means a complete change in our life. There is to be a revolution . . . a turning round. We must turn to God as a child turns to his father. It is that sort of turning . . . complete trust, complete faith.

A converted Christian is called a 'believer'; a good Jew is a 'righteous man'—what he does determines his relationship to God. A pious pagan Greek was one who knew—knowledge was to bring him union with his gods. But with Christians, it is the certainty that God is our Father, and that Jesus Christ is our Lord, that shows our conversion.

That is what converts us, brings about the extraordinary change. There is no more fear. We are no longer obsessed by our sense of guilt. We are a part of the Church, members of Christ, children of God and inheritors of the Kingdom of Heaven. We are members of a community of forgiven sinners; we are of the Communion of Saints.

So long as we stay converted, we shall be drawing closer to God; and the longer we stay that way the more difficult will it be to escape. Being close to God (who contains everything, never let it be forgotten) means that we shall not feel the need of creatures. We shall no doubt enjoy them still, perhaps even more than we did before, but we shall not need them. It may still hurt to have to part with people and things, but we shall not feel despairing about it. We shall not say, "I cannot live without you". We may not feel like living without them, but we shall want, as long as we are still converted, to do what God wants. He may take nothing from us, if the things or people we love do not take our love from him.

There is no violent effort needed, just a look

inwards towards God, and away from the people and things that distract. Then we shall love and not desire; we shall adore and not lust. That is all, only a loving look towards the Father. Every time we remember to do that, we shall be one of the children of whom is the Kingdom of Heaven (Matthew 19 : 14).

God is so compelling; and he attracts to purify and refine, to make sensitive and appreciative. He is the centre of truth to which we are being drawn.

The great heresy is to believe that we are centres of anything. We can never be a centre. We are points on a circumference, an ever decreasing circumference.

Nothing can prevent our approach to the centre, unless we belong to some creature that we believe to be a centre.

The whole of our attention should be fixed on remembering that we are God's, as effortlessly as we know all day that we belong to our human beloved. This continual remembering brings its own reward. It brings the grace of, in the end, finding it easy, if only we will draw back from the people and things that distract us. Not all people and things distract us from God; some remind us of him very forcibly.

But when there seems a likelihood of being blinded by passion or desire, the only way to keep control is to hurry back into the presence of God, who is always with us, however turbulent the blood, however dry the mouth. That is the only way of putting out the fire, without in any way adding fuel for future conflagrations.

# XII

## ACTIVE PEACE

# ACTIVE PEACE

When anyone has tried faithfully to love in this way, he is astonished at the hold God has on him. The Presence of God becomes a natural state with him. This is the result of habit. Peace and relaxation can be ours as the result of habitually loving God.

Prayer will turn more and more into an alert and watchful silence; alert and watchful in the same way as the trusting lover misses nothing of the beauty and charm of the beloved. And this Beloved rewards the trusting lover with a sort of love that brings an indescribable happiness and peace with it: a veritable bliss that the great lovers of God tell us grows and grows until there is no consummation possible but the final triumphant leap into the eternal, unchanging Presence.

God does it all. He says, "Be still, and know that I am God" (Psalm 46 : 10). But we refuse to believe that our own efforts are useless. We must be useless and know it, so that God can pick us up and use us. He knows what we are good for, for he made us. We must treasure every gift and skill that he has given us, and always be ready and willing to be put to his use; and we shall be very surprised at what he can do with us, at the mysterious successes that attend our God-impelled actions.

It is clear to anyone who has ever been in the stillness where he knows that God is God, that it is not idleness or inaction, but a secrecy in which something is growing, germinating. It is the very opposite of apathy; the opposite of a silence where there is nothing to say. It is the silence where one cannot speak, for no words could add to the fullness of the meaning of the stillness. It is an active peace, where the self learns that it really does not count at all, unless it is to become something for God to fill and use.

At the beginning of our prayer, we may find it necessary to use words—loving words perhaps, or just "Jesus!", and sometimes—it all depends—"Have mercy!" But one knows what to say when one loves.

The place in us where God dwells cannot be taken by assault; it is part of the Kingdom of Heaven and can only be conquered by love.

God wants us to be simple and childlike. We could easily attain to this active peace, if we were not afraid of the demands God would make on us. All we have to do is to put ourselves into his loving hands. We run no risks. There is nothing to be afraid of, for he is Love.

# XIII

## REST

# REST

WHEN people begin to pray like this, they find that they slip into it quite naturally and more and more frequently; it is almost unceasing prayer. Outside things do not interrupt it. This is when it becomes possible to say, "I live, yet not I, but Christ liveth in me" (Galatians 2 : 20). The only way to find him is to turn in towards him.

It even becomes easy to be good, almost natural and spontaneous. Rottenness and untruth do not seem to be able to touch us.

We shall always be ready to make our confession and communion; the day will have been a preparation for it. We have been waiting for God all the time, and if he wants to come to us in another way, or if we must receive him in another way, we are ready.

The expectant and adoring heart is the most fitting place for the Lord to rest, in whatever way he chooses to visit his child.

# XIV

## WE HAVE TO LISTEN IF WE WANT TO PRAY

# WE HAVE TO LISTEN IF WE
# WANT TO PRAY

ANY sort of prayer that we make presupposes that we have at some time or other been listening to the word of God.

Most of us have heard his word over and over again. Our faith rests upon what he has said about himself; and we know that no relationship of any sort would be possible between God and us, did he not make the first advances.

God once spoke to Abram, and when Abram answered, a never-ending dialogue began. (Genesis 15.) The whole Bible is a continuation of that conversation. Even Jesus was only carrying on the conversation that once began when God addressed himself to Abram.

Jesus Christ is the Word of God, and we have to be passive and attentive if we want to hear him. We have to forget ourselves and our little kingdoms, and listen attentively. That is the way to be beautiful with the only beauty that he sees.

Strange as it may seem, it is in the silence that we can speak to him best: in the silence of meditation, when we respond to him; in questioning silence, when we wait for him to explain to us what it is he wants us to do or know; in troubled silence, when we know that we are confronted with our Judge, and our whole life is lit up and we see it for what it is, and God invites us to change our ways; in the silence which is a cry for help, when we see that we cannot possibly do what he is asking us, and realize that it is only he who can give us the strength; and in awed silence, when we see him as he allows himself to be seen, and we quail at our own nothingness, and then discover that he is asking us to live as his sons and daughters.

We need times of outward silence, if we are to know the inward sort. Some lucky ones can always find it, but all must be on the look-out for the silent moment that is possible, when no one and nothing can get at them; and it nearly always is possible to find it some time or somewhere.

If by our stupidity or faithlessness we get separated from our only Centre, and thus dissipated, it is of vital importance that we turn gently inwards again. He is always there whatever we do. This is the way to keep the spirit of prayer with us all through the day. The few minutes or hours we spend on our knees are pretty useless unless we try to live with God all our other minutes.

# XV

## WHAT GOD SEES IN US

# WHAT GOD SEES IN US

AT the end of each day we should take a little look at ourselves—at the progress we have made towards God—or away from him. It need only take a moment. We usually know pretty exactly the direction our day has taken.

If we have been trying to live in the presence of God all through the day (and it is important to emphasize this, because what follows does not apply very much to people who have not been trying), it will be God far more than ourselves who will enlighten us. If we make strenuous great scouring efforts to clean up our consciences, we are more than likely to get things wrong.

If we have been trying to leave ourselves in the hand of God, it is only sensible to leave our self-examination to him, too.

A conscience that has been entrusted to God grows extraordinarily tender. It knows and blushes at the smallest deviation from love. It knows when it is denying its Love. This is true sorrow for sin; and we may expect to have that agonizing and loving penance inflicted on us that Peter had: "Lovest thou me?" (John 21 : 16, 17). And if we have been trying, we too shall be able to answer truthfully, "Thou knowest that I love thee."

One of the strangest things that happens to trusting, loving souls is that, although they have been living lives far different from the sort of life their Love lived when he was on earth, they cannot, for the life of them, think of anything to confess. If this should happen, the matter for confession very probably is, "I know I haven't been what God wants me to be, but I can't think of where I've gone wrong."

We shall always be ready for confession and communion, if we have been living constantly with God. The certain knowledge that the Kingdom of God is within us, prepares us for everything. Nothing will catch us off our guard, not even death.

# XVI

## PRAYING WITH A BOOK OR
## WITH THE LIPS

# PRAYING WITH A BOOK OR
# WITH THE LIPS

SOME people find it easier to pray with a book. Some people pray with a gospel open in front of them. But if, while reading, we find that we are aware of God, then often it is wiser to stop reading, and rest in the Beloved.

It is very important to know how little to read, and how often to re-read the little that has been read.

It may happen that what we read in the Bible may seem to have nothing to say to us, or even to have no meaning at all. We should not be too quick to leave even those strange words. The corn of wheat has to stay in the earth a long time before it yields its harvest; and the word of God has to stay a long time in us before it produces all its fruit. So let us keep even this word. You never know. We ought to be like Mary, who when she did not understand what was being said, "kept all these sayings in her heart" (Luke 2:51).

Our prayer lies just as much in the word of God received (in fact that is one whole half of prayer) as it does in our response to that word. We must be waiting to hear what God has to say to us.

We should never force ourselves to use words when we pray. God may be waiting for our silence. There are, of course, times when it is our duty to pray with words, when we should be disobedient if we didn't, but in other cases it is better not to be tied to set forms of prayer, but to allow the Spirit to lead us where he wills. Everything will be included in that.

# XVII

## PRAYING FOR OTHERS

# PRAYING FOR OTHERS

IT seems to happen to many, after they have been trying to pray for some years, that they find they cannot pray for others as easily as they used to.

This may be a sign that God wants to take over. He must know better than we ever can what is truly best for the people and causes we want to pray for.

This whole situation has been admirably explained in a certain Prologue to Intercession that the Cowley Fathers suggest: "I commend to Thy loving care and mercy, Almighty and Everlasting God, all for whom I ought to pray. Thou knowest their every need—but I, how little do I know? Holy Father, merciful Saviour, gracious Spirit, One eternal God, take my ignorant prayer, in union with the prayer of Our Lady and all the company of Heaven, and arise and do, through the merits and mediation of Jesus Christ, our only Lord and Saviour. Amen."

So, if you have many people to pray for, it is one idea to make a methodical list of them in some little handy book, and just go through the list as often as you can: some parts perhaps daily, some weekly, and so on; just saying the names in the presence of your Love and theirs, whether they know he is or not. He knows what they need.

The very fact that you have got the little book somehow, that you have remembered the person, written down the name, and repeated the name with your lips in God's presence, is some sort of love.

Prayer does not go anywhere unless there is some sort of love behind it. We cannot always feel loving, but we can always do the loving thing.

A husband may not always feel like making his wife a cup of tea first thing in the morning in a cold kitchen, but if he does it for the good reason he is a loving husband.

The farther we go along the way the more

people and things we shall find we have to pray
for. The time may well come when we shall
know that all we are able to do is to hold them
up on our hearts in the presence of God, and
leave them there. The Holy Spirit will keep his
promise, for we shall never know how to pray
as we ought, but he will pray instead of us 'with
sighs too deep for words' (Romans 8 : 26
American RSV).

# XVIII

## THE BAD PATCH

# THE BAD PATCH

IF we should ever drift away from remembering that God has chosen us for his home, if we begin to be dissipated or self-indulgent or generally frivolous, the thing to do is to turn inwards again; and to do it quickly, directly it becomes clear or (hideous thought) when we remember that we have got lost.

We must return to our Father as soon as we realize where we are, and take whatever unpleasant sensations he is pleased to give us.

The thing to avoid at all costs is being annoyed with ourselves or worried about our state. That only means that our pride and self-esteem has been touched. We do not like to know what we are like. The more we despair the feebler we get. We are not being sorry that we have not loved, but sorry that we are not as good as we thought.

If we are really humble, we shall expect to be full of faults and failings. The more pitiable we see ourselves to be, the closer we shall press inwards towards God, so that he can more easily use his unfailing strength to set us on the right way again.

# XIX

## TROUBLE

# TROUBLE

To fight temptations and distractions is really not the best way of setting about it. It usually only makes things worse; and it always does, if the struggle draws away the soul from God.

The best and safest way is to turn from the bad thing and draw nearer to God.

It is foolish for children to fight dragons; it is far better for them to run home and hide their heads in Mother's lap. Then they are quite certain they are safe.

It we attempt to attack our spiritual enemies, more often than not we shall get hurt, if not actually beaten. But if we return to the presence of God, we cannot help but find strength and protection.

It is wonderful how evil disappears at the name of JESUS.

# XX

## THE LIVELY SACRIFICE

# THE LIVELY SACRIFICE

NOT all sacrifices have to do with garlanded beasts, little square altars, flowers, and smoking entrails. The Book of Common Prayer speaks of a 'sacrifice of praise and thanksgiving', which sounds like another name for love.

We long to be able to praise truthfully and to be truly thankful for the creature we love. It is not always feasible. Yet we try to sacrifice ourselves to our beloveds.

The sacrifice a lover makes, seems to him, at the start at any rate, to have little or nothing to do with death. To him it is something full of life, even life-bringing, truly 'lively'.

The perfect example of the Lover's sacrifice can be seen in the stable at Bethlehem. There we can look at Humanity emptied of everything that will prevent It serving the Word of God.

That is what we want to be like in our own trivial way. If we succeed at all, we shall be proportionately fuller of life, more delightful to God.

When we allow God to be 'in the midst of us' as he wants to be, he will gradually melt away everything that hinders him from working in and through us.

It is the power of the Thing that possesses us that destroys our stubbornness and self-satisfaction. For instance, a *great* outpouring of divine power seems to be necessary to make us considerate and sympathetic with an inopportune seeker for our help. It is in such small things that we refuse to accept God. But when we do accept him, it is the perfect Christian sacrifice. We are possessed and possessing, truly loving and being loved.

This is what we mean to do when we say, 'I believe in God'. There are only two truths in our faith: *God is all*, and *I am nothing*. So when we pray, we pour out our soul before God, and the moment we do that, he who hates emptiness fills us with himself.

We none of us know how to pray, but emptied of self and filled with God we can hope for completion.

There is nothing to fear, nothing to lose, and yet we dare not leap out of our selfishness into the arms of Love. We think we shall be cheated. We think we shall not have our rights. We are afraid of the demands he will make. But when we dare, the reward is infinitely beyond anything we have imagined. This is the pearl of great price (Matthew 13 : 46); this is the hidden treasure (Matthew 13 : 44); this is the well of living water springing up into everlasting life (John 4 : 14). This is how to adore God in spirit and in truth (John 4 : 23).

He never takes anything from us. We have nothing to give him; but he loads us with his loveliness. He can make us truly alive, if only we will sacrifice our hindering self.

# XXI

## WHAT HAPPENS

# WHAT HAPPENS

THIS business of being silent and turning inwards when we pray has nothing to do with inactivity, wool-gathering, or gazing into the middle distance. It is the supreme activity. It is the activity of the Creator of action. It is God the Holy Spirit at work. We have allowed him to work in us, as Mary did. We are preparing ourselves to be led by God wherever he wills. We are ready to act through grace alone.

When we worry and fret and flap about what we have to do, and our preparations for doing it, and the preparations for our preparations, then we feel very busy. Therefore the freedom that comes from acting under the grace of God may seem as if we were doing nothing about anything at all; but our preparation lies in our attention and alertness and sensitiveness to God. We shall not be used, never forget, unless we are trying all the day long to do what we know is the will of God for us. Prayer is not only made on the knees.

Those who live by grace seem so quick, so natural, so peaceful, so spontaneous. And they get through an enormous amount of work. Television appearances, broadcasting, a vast correspondence and public speaking seem only to leave some of them with more time for their neighbour. We all know busy Christians who always have time; it is because they let God work in them, and he is eternal. They live and move and have their being in him (Acts 17 : 28).

To be like a child dependent on its Father is the reason we were created. If we are to get back to the unity and simplicity of Adam before the Fall, if we are to escape the new diseases of the brain and nerves, it is absolutely vital that we make up our minds to behave as we were created to behave. A piano will never be happy while it is trying to be a guitar.

We shall not get left behind if we concentrate on being one with God. If we are moved by his Spirit, we shall be infinitely active, and with an activity very different from our own.

We were created in his image, and since that

7

image has been obscured we must wait for the Spirit to be breathed into us again, as it was in the beginning. Only God can restore his image in us. Jesus said he had the life in himself, and he longs to give it to us (John 5 : 26). That is what he came for. We can only make room for it if we suppress self. "If any man be in Christ, he is a new creature: old things are passed away; behold, all things are become new" (2 Cor. 5 : 17).

We are to be as active as Jesus was. He is the standard set us.

When we begin to seek God in our hearts, first we fall under the influence of his attraction; later we cannot bear to be separated from him, and any wilful straying from him seems an impossible agony too terrible to think of; in the end, there is union with him: the prodigal returns. We return to our source.

The Spirit's 'sighs too deep for words' have been heard.

# XXII

## TURNED TO GOD

# TURNED TO GOD

In the early days of our attraction towards God, we need to remind ourselves pretty constantly of his presence.

Perhaps in the very earliest days we are so astounded and delighted at our discovery of him, and so surprised that we did not know it all before, that the consciousness of his nearness to us is with us practically all the time.

But this may be just 'gilt on the gingerbread': it may be largely to do with our feelings, and little to do with the will.

As time goes on, and the novelty of our great experience wears off, we find a need to turn to him deliberately. We discover that we turn from him more or less wilfully, and then we have to use the will again to bring our consciousness back to him. He has been with us all the time, but we have forgotten: forgotten what he wants us to do, forgotten how he wants us to love.

We shall probably find that we have to recall our wandering will by some quite deliberate act: some trusting, loving, repentant word.

This state of things may last a long time. We are so at the mercy of our feelings. We find them so much easier to live with than with our will. But every time we use our will to bring us back to God the dissipations grow less frequent.

The time will come, we are told, when we shall live so constantly in the presence of God that we shall never need to remind ourselves of him. Then our turnings to him will only be the look of love and trust that lovers know instinctively how and when to use.

Our love for God will run on the same lines as our love for our human beloved. We are human, and human love is all we can know. But no other human love can be as perfect and satisfying as the human love we have for the Divine Lover.

He is called a jealous God, which means that he demands complete fidelity; but when we try to give him that we find all the lesser loves take their true place with us in him.

He never asks us to give up our best and most beautiful things. If they are good and beautiful they are in some way reflections of him, and so we must keep them.

All love must be directed by the will and brain. If it is not, when we cease to feel, when we get no kick, when there is no sensation of love left, we say the *affaire* is over, or our marriage has broken up, or my prayer means nothing to me any more.

When we talk like that we have got love all wrong. True love, given a chance, must last. It was always meant to last. It is part of God.

When attraction, sensation or feeling stops,

then faithfulness, self-sacrifice and trust must step in. They become the only way left to express love. They are love. The saints do not distinguish between faithfulness and love, or self-sacrifice and love, or trust and love.

This seems like a meditation on the perfect married couple, but that, *in excelsis*, is how a soul wholly turned to God behaves.

# XXIII

## HOW DULL ARE THE SERVICES AT YOUR CHURCH?

# HOW DULL ARE THE SERVICES
## AT YOUR CHURCH?

To live this way of prayer might be the very sort of evangelism that is needed.

Every member of the Church of England is expected to go to church on Sunday. It is one of his primary duties. But the man who knows that God lives in him, could not stay away when he knows that the God who reigns in his heart and in heaven, is coming too to the altars of his Church to offer his people the Bread of Life.

There is some mysterious divine longing in Our Lord's heart which seems to find satisfaction when his little ones are round his Table.

He has asked us to do this in remembrance of him. In this act he wants to be called back among his loves in a special way. No lover of his could refuse to go.

Wherever God is spoken to or praised or talked about, there also should his lovers be.

Mattins and Evensong can hardly be dull to one who loves. If the services are poorly attended there is a certain way to make them less so: to go ourselves. If they seem dull it is perhaps our fault. We may have forgotten that we are there to praise and speak to and listen to our Love among the other Christ-bearers. He promised he would be where two or three gathered together for the sake of him.

It is the old, old story. The Church can only be perfectly holy when all its members are holy; and it is impossible for us to be really holy outside the Church, Christ's Body. We need each other. The Church will not be perfect without the contribution to its perfection that only I can make. I shall not reach the full height of holiness that God intended for me if I separate myself from him in any way.

We cannot help but grow in recollection if we pray and praise our indwelling Love in and with him in his Church. We hear him speak, we hear his word explained. For us, who know how vital it is for the soul's good to be humble and attentive, there can be no sermon without a revelation for us. A sermon depends little upon the preacher for its effect on the hearers. It is the word of God addressed to his people.

If we know the happiness of the Kingdom of Heaven within us, it should be our delight to pass on the good news. We might be able to make one other long to be where God longs for us to be on his Day.

# XXIV

## THE END

# THE END

GOD wills we should be one in him: as he was in Jesus and Jesus in him.

Nothing that we can do can bring about this supreme and unutterable good. We can be ready and waiting for God to do with us what he likes, but that is all.

What COULD we do? He is pure and we are impure. He is simplicity—One—and we are so terribly complicated. The best we can think of, in our ignorance, is the driving out of self. If we are truly selfless, God can do the rest.

Self-sufficiency and therefore pride are the foundations of all our complications. We have to wait in stillness and peace for God to restore us to the purity man once knew at his first creation. That is what we must will, for God will never rob us of our power to will. We cannot love without that.

Starting out on this short way to God was a wonderful moment for us; the end is to be unspeakable bliss, completion, being what we can sometimes dimly guess we were intended to be: utterly simple again. There is every likelihood that the way between will be full of strange adventures, each one taking from us something that would hinder our further progress. It is those adventures that we fear. It is they which hold us back. We dare not face our little Calvaries, even though we know that Easter lies on the other side.

Jesus would not have made this way for us if there had been any danger in it. If we start out on it, we shall find it the loveliest road we have ever known. It is suited to everyone. No one can fail to experience the peace and certainty of being on the right and only way. We are on the way to enjoy God himself—not his gifts, but him himself; for nothing but God can satisfy our immense capacity for happiness. He longs to give himself to us. That is why he made us. If only we would leave it to him, he would show us how easy he is to love.